Why Are They Like That?
Whites

*Questions you've dared to ask, answered
by real people, celebrities and experts*

A book series based on the award-winning
sharing project that's captured worldwide
attention helping people in their personal,
social and business relationships

Phillip J. Milano

For Robin, Jacob, Lucas and Ben

Publisher:
Y Forum
yforum@yforum.com

ISBN: 978-1-07-917242-3

Cover and interior layout by Sandy Weber,
Key 3 Creative, Jacksonville, Florida
Cover photo credit: Rawpixel. Stock photo for illustrative purposes
only; any person depicted is a posed model.

Content based in part on the popular Y? sharing project and Dare
to Ask column

Find out more about the author, upcoming books and speeches at
www.phillipmilano.com, www.facebook.com/PhillipJMilano or
@PhillipMilano.

Books In This Series

Why Are They Like That? Blacks

Why Are They Like That? Whites

Why Are They Like That? Hispanics

Why Are They Like That? Asians

Why Are They Like That? Gay Men

Why Are They Like That? Lesbians

Why Are They Like That? Women

Why Are They Like That? Men

Why Are They Like That? Rich and Poor

Why Are They Like That? Religious (or not)

Why Are They Like That? Disabled People

Why Are They Like That? Young and Old

Praise for the Y? sharing project and the book "I Can't Believe You Asked That!" (Perigee)

"Milano is quietly revolutionizing cross-cultural communication..."
- Pulitzer Prize-winning columnist Leonard Pitts

"If you've ever hesitated to ask a question because you think it might be considered insensitive or impolitic, now is your chance ... Nothing is considered out of bounds..."
- CNN Headline News

"(It) tells more about who we are and how we feel about each other than you're likely to learn from a dozen sociology texts…"
- Washington Post News Service

"Mr. Milano has dared to open the field of debate to the maximum…"
- Le Monde, Paris

"(A) remarkable contribution to cross-cultural understanding…"
- The (London) Guardian

"A truly rare achievement ... has the potential to have a profound impact on the way we all see and understand each other..."
- Playboy magazine

"It's an incredible book. It diffuses everything ... Nothing is off limits, and the questions have that childlike honesty to them..."
- Dee Snider, Twisted Sister; host, "Dee Snider Radio"

"A take-no-prisoners attitude prevails between the volume's covers . . . This book is hard to put down..."
- Midwest Book Review

"A+ (highest rating) ... Everything you wanted to know but were afraid to ask gets tackled here ..."
- Entertainment Weekly

CONTENTS

Introduction

Why Are They Like That? is a series of books based on an award-winning worldwide sharing project in which real people, experts and celebrities talk about things that make us different from each other. Silly things. Sad things. Funny things. Profound things.

Read with an open mind and we believe that by the time you're finished you'll have a much better understanding of how to make more and real friends, money and love. It's that simple.

Why? Because this isn't about trying to get ahead with diversity training. We are well beyond that. According to the Census Bureau, by 2050 the United States will have no racial or ethnic minority.

No, this is about moving past talking about how to understand each other to talking to each other. Right now.

That's why there's no agenda to these books other than getting the conversation going. We can discuss studies and methods for elevating social consciousness all we want, but there is no substitute for real dialogue.

That's where Why Are They Like That? stands apart from other books on the topic. You will see how people talk about their real differences of race, religion, sex, disability and more.

The success of the approach is proven: It's based on the ground-breaking Y? website project, blog and column that have attracted millions of visitors and worldwide media attention.

Our hope is that by reading, you will become more comfortable asking and answering the questions yourself, expecting the unexpected in return and helping change the ground rules for how we learn from and about each other. To that end, we wrap up each book in the series with our O.U.T.L.O.U.D. Method for Dialogue, with tips to help you get your own conversations started. Ultimately, that is what this effort is all about.

After all, if you want to make more friends, money and love, you better know the people you're talking to, selling to or opening to. Knowledge isn't just power. It's all power.

Enjoy.

Phillip J. Milano
Founder, Y?

Are all women (even whites) gettin' bigger and bigger?

They asked:

When I was young, I never saw fat white women. Now, everywhere I go, I see out-of-shape white women. Many of them, especially their legs, are larger than NFL players. What happened? Is it their diet, or are they just lazy?

— Dorothy, black female, Jacksonville

You said:

We're lazy, our cities lack green spaces to exercise, we watch too much TV, corporations push high-fructose corn syrup down our throats, school lunches are too starchy, it's not even safe for kids to walk to school so they sit on their butts all the time . . . And big pharma and its expensive drugs for type II diabetes and cholesterol couldn't be happier.

— D.L., female, Los Angeles

I'm not sure that it is limited to white women, but sadly I think it is a sign of the times. Everything is about convenience and rushing to stay ahead.

— S.E., 31, white female, Jacksonville

We found:

For years, we've all assumed this affliction was unique to white ladies. Didn't Robert Plant seal the deal when he penned the seminal Led Zeppelin lyrics "I don't know but I been told, a big-legged woman ain't got no soul"?

Now comes Beth Carlton Tohill to knock down the myth.

Tohill, lead epidemiologist for the Centers for Disease Control and an expert on obesity, stunned us by revealing that women of all colors can be fat.

In fact, "Historically, a higher percentage of non-Hispanic black women have been obese or overweight, followed by Hispanic women, and then non-Hispanic whites," she said.

But, the real skinny is that all categories of women are gaining weight, Tohill notes. CDC surveys show that the percent of black women who are obese has risen from 37 to 51, and the percent of white women who are fat has climbed from 23 to 31.

"People are more sedentary, they're using TV remote controls, and those modern conveniences are adding up," Tohill said. "There are also more inexpensive, high-calorie foods and sugary beverages."

As far as more black women being overweight: in a study by Yale University public health professor Tene T. Lewis and colleagues that looked at obesity in women, researchers commented that "research suggests there is less stigma associated with being overweight or obese for African-American compared with white women." They also noted that "compared with white women, African-American women report less of a 'drive for thinness' and tend to prefer 'curvaceous,' normal weight vs. thin body ideals."

Tohill agreed there's no hard science behind the weight differences, but "there is a perception that it is more culturally desirable among black women and men not to be thin . . .

"But, we are all getting used to everyone being larger."

What's all the fuss about good grammar with white people?

They asked:

Why are white people so dogmatic about grammar? Good grammar isn't linked to intelligence.

— Nia C., 30, black, Chicago

You said:

I admit that proper grammar is important to me and that I form an at least partially negative impression of people who use poor grammar. I agree that good grammar does not equate with intelligence, but poor grammar does not suggest someone is particularly intelligent.

— J.M., 37, white male, Conn.

Grammar is not linked to intelligence, but that's the perception. And it doesn't matter the race of the language-mangler. Speaking non-standard English can give the impression the speaker is ill-educated. As an employer, I look for people who can communicate well and who will represent my company in a professional and positive way.

— Maria, 50, white, Raleigh, N.C.

I proudly speak and write American English, do it to the best of my abilities, judge people on their merits, not the color of their skin, love my country and avoid people who want to destroy it, and love my private-school college degree and six-figure job. Can I get a woohoo?

— MrPatrick, Florida

If I need an urban dictionary or a primer on the meaning of Web-based acronyms to read and understand a post or commentary, I discount the content entirely and move on. A poorly written argument full of grammatical and/or spelling errors suggests the writer is either intellectually lazy, poorly educated or both.

— JaxJLB, white female, Jacksonville

10

My black friends who are educated and have excellent grammar turn it on and off like a switch, depending on who they are talking to.

— *Friedman, white male*

Being a substitute teacher, I could ask one student to answer a question and almost cringe at the grammar while they're speaking, but another student speaks so eloquently. And this is a white and black child, respectively. It's all in the education, and whoever is doing the upbringing of a child.

— *Mterry2216, 36, white female*

Has nothing to do with race. Stupid, classless, uneducated people don't speak correct English.

— *Brpatton*

We found:

Bill White writes the "Grammar Police" column for The Morning Call in Allentown, Pa. He's no Caucasian snob. For this guy, stressing good grammar isn't about looking down on others, whatever their race. It's about holding to a standard.

"I'm fine with casual use and slang in the right situations, and I recognize that language evolves, but people will judge you in a not-positive way if you're sloppy with spelling and grammar, and it shows a certain disrespect that you didn't take the trouble to proofread something you sent."

While street dialect is OK among friends, White draws the line at teaching something like Ebonics in the schools.

"I don't know that I want to say there is no standard, and talk however you want. We're better off knowing that standard so we can communicate in any circle."

And there are payoffs to standard English, he joked.

"My own family can't get 'lay' and 'lie' correct. They tell the dog to go lay down, but the dog responds better to me because I use correct grammar."

So what color is your welcome mat?

They asked:

To white people: Would you invite a black person to your home? Have you?

— *Frederick, Jacksonville*

You said:

I'm a 48-year-old female with children, and all their friends were welcome in my home as long as they behaved. What a weird question. Get over yourself.

— *Colleen, white, Orange Park, Fla.*

I don't like having stupid people over for dinner. They come in all colors.

— *Georgia, Lodi, Calif.*

Of course I've invited black people to my home. I wish we lived in a world where this question was patently ridiculous.

— *Jorge, 52, Hispanic, Jacksonville, Fla.*

My guest list for my 11th birthday sleepover consisted of two white girls, the one Hispanic girl in our class and four black girls. It's called "friendship." Get familiar with the concept.

— *A., 38, Kansas City, Mo.*

I have many times, but avoid inviting African-Americans who always remind others they are black. For instance, the famous comment "I'm the only black person here." Like we didn't notice. Now you've made people uncomfortable. That's not a relaxing evening, and you will not be invited back.

— *Kristin, 44, Ponte Vedra Beach, Fla.*

We found:

We're just glad nobody gets ruffled by these questions.

But if any white people were to get defensive, it might be because they tend to overestimate the amount of true, cross-racial interaction they have, said University of Texas journalism professor Robert Jensen, who studies race and authored "The Heart of Whiteness: Confronting Race, Racism and White Privilege."

"A lot of white people, intellectually we can say all people are equal, but how much have we really internalized that?" he said.

Cowardice, housing patterns, church habits and other factors have led to ingrained racial segregation, which can be monumental to overcome in one's personal life, Jensen said.

"You might have black colleagues at work, but your personal world is still overwhelmingly white. We're in a society that still reflects a white supremacist distribution of wealth and power, as well as our own struggles with internalized racism."

Non-whites are essentially forced to interact with whites all the time, but for whites, it's mostly a choice whether to integrate — and therein lies the challenge.

"Moderate white America still finds it uncomfortable to bump up against these realities," said Jensen, adding that class and culture are huge variables in whether whites accept minorities.

He gave Barack Obama's election as an example, saying it would have been different had he not been light-skinned, Ivy-educated and "soothing to white people."

"If he'd framed his politics as based on racial justice, he wouldn't have gotten elected. Imagine if he had come from a black urban environment, and had a cadence to his speech out of Harlem or the Deep South. Do you think he would've gotten elected?"

13

Do white guys just come up lame on the basketball court?

They asked:

I started at guard in high school and got offered a scholarship. Now when I play basketball at a gym and there are mostly black players, I can't get the ball passed to me because I am white. Why is that?

— John, Jacksonville, N.C.

You said:

You suck. The only time you get the ball is when you're open, because most of you guys can shoot.

— Chris, 17, Matteson, Ill.

If I had a guy who could consistently drop threes and help the team, I wouldn't care if he was green.

— Timand, black, Miami

White guys are a liability on the court. You have to try and showcase your skills.

—Jason, 23, black, Chicago

A lot of black men come from backgrounds that have imbued them with a deep-seated hatred of white men.

— C., 41, white, Wyoming

The basketball court is many times the only guaranteed controlled space for a black man, and therefore he will only respect you there if you earn it as he had to.

— Sharell, 21, black, Summit Argo, Ill.

We found:

Let's slowly (but with excellent outside range) walk through the stereotypes as described by Reuben May, a Texas A&M sociologist who studied boys high school basketball and wrote "Living through the Hoop: High School Basketball, Race, and the American Dream." They are: Black players are faster, white dudes don't elevate, blacks are more athletic and whites play a team-aspect game while blacks are all about taking it right to you.

Ingrained perceptions about those stereotypes — especially the latter ones — mean it can be a bummer on-court for a white guy trying to fit in with a bunch of black players, said May, a former research fellow at Harvard.

"It's a cultural thing," said May, who is black. "They can be preoccupied with showmanship and reluctant to share the ball, and so there is less fluid team play."

In their defense, they often grow up hearing a lot about one-on-one NBA "matchups," and also may feel that because they're black, they must own the court, he said.

Here's what white-guy John needs to do:

"If he gets the ball and passes it, he's suggesting he wants to just be part of a whole. But if he gets it and says 'I'm going to take this guy,' he'll be more accepted. Impose yourself on the context. He needs to be like them and not be a team player. As a guard, he was likely appreciated for managing the ball well and taking good shots. That crap doesn't fly in pickup. Can you outdo the guy guarding you?"

If he can, preconceptions about his abilities will melt.

"He'll be accepted," May said. "Now, they might still incorporate some stereotype into their talk, like 'Yeah that's my white friend, but he can play...' "

And the showy guys (black or white) who make it to college teams and the NBA? They quickly add team play to their show — or they won't get minutes, May added.

One for the road: Can folks get a smile from a white driver?

They asked:

It used to be you could get a smile and wave from your fellow driver regardless of color, but now it seems if the person pulling up beside me is white, they purposefully turn their heads away ("Eek! A black!"). Especially white guys — if they're trying to "check me out," if they see me looking back, it's "Oops it's a Negro," and they accelerate away. Am I trying to read too much into this?

— Pamela, black, Jacksonville

You said:

It could be they are afraid of being perceived as doing the wrong thing, and then getting attacked. With all the diversity training I get at work, it makes me think three times before I ask any question of a black man or woman, out of fear of legal entanglements.

— Burt, 48, Irvine, Calif.

I can't say it's so good in Connecticut, either. But I promise that if you're a good-looking woman of any color (or age) driving around me, I'll be scoping you out with appreciation.

— Chris, Windsor, Conn.

I found black/white relations [were] much better after the election of Obama. I noticed by the day after his election that blacks returned my smiles when perhaps in the past they hadn't.

— Dot, white, Los Angeles

White people do that to everyone. It doesn't matter what race you are. Try waving hello first and see how they respond. If they don't wave back, it doesn't make them a racist, just a jerk.

— Matt, Baltimore

We found:

Sociology professor Barbara Trepagnier, who is white, has done many focus groups in her home about racism with white people who don't think they're racist. You have to admire a high-squirm threshold.

One thing she found was that some white folks said they felt anxious around black people — primarily black women — who they felt just didn't like them.

"They felt that they won't go out of their way to be friendly, unless a white person is friendly first," said Trepagnier, a professor at Texas State University-San Marcos and author of "Silent Racism: How Well-Meaning White People Perpetuate the Racial Divide."

Keep in mind it's their perception, she noted — just as Pamela's question above is based on her perception and can't be stated as an overall fact or trend just yet.

But, if our questioner is on to something, it may be that white people are nervous about blacks gaining power.

"That's a kind of racism that's been repressed for a long time," she said.

"There may be that suspicion that something is going to get taken away from us. It breaks my heart."

Is NPR for rich, white, liberals only?

They asked:

Does anyone else think National Public Radio is the voice of all the white, rich, liberals (mainly women) ... with nothing better to do than brag about their most recent "knitting in Manhattan" idiocy or lame adventure in Europe?

— *Jerry R., 30, Indianapolis*

You said:

Yes ... just as loads of others think other media outlets are run by and for arrogant, narrow-minded rich Republican white men.

— *Julia, 32, white, St. Louis*

If someone said the same thing about a station that catered primarily to black Americans (which I suspect you are), you'd probably be first in line to defend it!

— *Rachel, 47, black, Australia*

NPR makes no secret about its political leanings, and often offers a balanced viewpoint on current issues.

— *Sheila, 30, white, Tampa*

Recently I heard an NPR interview with a guy from Metallica — hardly fits your whiny, pampered, female stereotype, eh?

— *Kristy, Denver*

Most of my "conscious" friends are people of color, consider themselves radicals and listen to and respect National Public Radio.

— *Damon, 27, black, Inglewood, Calif.*

NPR is a nice alternative for those of us tired of Rush Limbaugh, Sean Hannity, Mike Savage, et al. ... who remain the real whiny radio voices.

— *Sam, 23, white, Orlando*

We found:

In between listening to pledge drives in the car, we found out:

Watchdog group Media Matters moaned that NPR's own numbers showed it used right-leaning experts 63 percent of the time. A UCLA-University of Missouri study found NPR's political bent was close to "the average mainstream news outlet" — about the same as Time and U.S. News & World Report. A Roper poll found that U.S. adults surveyed felt 28 percent of NPR's content was liberal — lower than any other media organization besides Fox News. In the poll, 23 percent of respondents self-identified as liberal, 34 percent conservative.

Jeffrey Dvorkin, former NPR ombudsman who writes the media blog *Now The Details*, agreed it was a "fair knock" to say NPR programming doesn't cater to minorities and that its audience is overwhelmingly white. However, he said it isn't as liberal as some think. One survey put its audience at 52 percent liberal, 48 percent conservative, he said.

"As ombudsman I got as many complaints saying how conservative it was as how left wing," said Dvorkin, now Program Director for Journalism at the University of Toronto Scarborough and Executive Director of the Organization of News Ombudsmen. "I think their reporting was strongly leaning to the skeptical, regardless of who was in power."

One problem was that beginning in the '80s, right-leaning think tanks made it appear that much of the media was too liberal, he said.

"I remember asking one think-tanker if he really thought NPR was as left wing as he and fellow think-tankers said it was. And he said, 'No, we only do that to put you on the defensive.' And that's exactly what's happened: It's the politicization of information in America."

19

Is it in whites' genes to be forever in blue jeans?

They asked:

Why do white people always wear blue jeans?
> — *Danny W., black, Memphis*

You said:

Wow, you are right! That is all I buy for casual. I do admire the bold colors and accessories I see black people wearing, which are very beautiful.
> — *Gina, 46, white, Flint, Mich.*

White people like to fit in more. Jeans seem to be the uniform. I used to have a pair of black jeans and I found out later that whenever I wore them, people thought I was rebelling, or trying to be emo or Goth. I just thought they looked nice.
> — *Alison K., 16, white, Herndon, Va.*

Because they are so common, people probably just think of them first when deciding what to wear. It's probably similar to young black men and sagging pants.
> — *Lynne, Gainesville, Fla.*

I don't wear blue jeans, because they're seen everywhere, from the guy picking up your trash on the garbage truck to the young, hot Hollywood starlet.
> — *Bella, 35, Afro-Caribbean, Washington, D.C.*

I have friends of many different backgrounds and ethnic groups. We all wear blue jeans . . . they just feel and look good.
> — *Josh, 22, white, Bossier City, La.*

Jeans . . . are forgiving and last for years. I can shop for hours trying to find decent trousers, or I can try on a couple of jeans and be out in under 10 minutes.
> — *CLR, 25, white female, Seattle*

We found:

There aren't huge bolts of data out there on denim preferences among races, but industry group Cotton Inc. did release this morsel: 73 percent of white men prefer denim over casual slacks, compared to 63 percent of black males.

Not a wide seam there — and that fits well for Paul Cavazos of Olah Inc. in New York, which tracks trends in jeans. He doesn't see whites monopolizing denim, or mainstream jeans stores locking in on one race.

"I'd be shocked if the Gap targets only Anglos; their ads are as diverse as they get."

But there may be demographic preferences. There's still some urban aesthetic for baggier jeans, though Cavazos says more urban black males are going for tighter-fitting jeans.

It may also be that urban males in particular don't put the focus on jeans when creating their overall look.

"Jeans can be a status symbol, but I don't think as much for urban men," he said. "They may spend more on tennis shoes, hoodies or coats . . . so it's a focus on other accessories."

For some women of color, on the other hand, finding the perfect pair of jeans is just more difficult — though more stores are focusing on jeans for differently proportioned figures.

Apple Bottoms, for example, a brand by rapper Nelly, makes jeans that "highlight and accentuate the curves of a woman," its website says. Other companies have popped up to appeal to women with wider hips but who have small waists — a style not always stocked by mass-market stores.

Red with anger: Fiery hair and a fiery temper?

They asked:

Why do they say people with red hair have a temper?
— *Marksam, 40, Rhyl, United Kingdom*

You said:

I had a school teacher who picked on me severely because she said she "knew" I had a bad temper because I have red hair. I'm one of the calmest people I know, although I have noticed that staying calm when someone wants an argument with you does annoy people greatly.

— *H., 24, London*

Being a redhead, people are prejudiced against me and treat me differently, and not in a good way. This pisses me off, and I let them know that, and they don't like it. So that makes me the bad guy in their eyes.

— *Jess, 40, male, Chicago*

My "temper" has nothing to do with the color of my hair. I will confess that I have, in the past, attempted to use it to "excuse" my behavior, but have learned not to because it can backfire. How? If I am really angry, I might not be listened to because it's just "an obvious reaction from a redhead — what can you expect?"
— *Vicci, Southampton, United Kingdom*

My grandmother still gets away with temper tantrums by blaming it on her "coloring" — even though it now comes out of a bottle!
— *B.B., 26, female, Edinburgh, United Kingdom*

We found:

Don't get mad about these interesting facts about redheads:

— They are more sensitive to pain and require more anesthetic for their operations, a study by anesthesiologist Edwin Liem at the University of Louisville found.

— According to a Washington Post article, a Clairol Color Attitudes Survey found 71 percent of redheads felt the word "bold" described them — compared to 47 percent of blondes.

— The red hair gene was discovered in 1995 by the lab of Jonathan Rees, now professor of dermatology at the University of Edinburgh. It may have popped up as recently as only 50,000 years ago. (A myth: Redheads, with their recessive gene, will be extinct in 100 years.)

So, why the temper talk?

According to red-haired Marion Roach, an NPR commentator and author of The Roots of Desire: The Myth, Meaning, and Sexual Power of Red Hair, the Greek philosophers of the fifth century B.C. said human temperaments were caused by four "humors," or bodily fluids, one of which was blood. Blood, being red, was associated with being sanguine. Redheads were thought to have this temperament. Eventually, though, it came to be thought of as just hot-headedness.

Also, many mythical and literary figures associated with evil or sin were portrayed as being red or redheaded — from Satan to Judas to Mary Magdalene to the demonlike Lilith. That didn't help matters.

Then there's the fact that redheads are just unusual, and people sometimes attach negative stereotypes to anything different, Roach said.

All the legends and stories don't bother her, though.

"I don't mind people thinking I'm bad-tempered. It's saved me some fights!"

23

Whites do it, blacks do it ... they all do it

They asked:

Are white girls more aggressive when it comes to sex?
— *TJ, 19, Puerto Rican male, Swarthmore, Pa.*

You said:

I think there may be a misconception among most girls my age that white girls are not supposed to be as "exciting" as those of other races, so maybe we are just trying to rebel against that image.
— *Kathryn, 15, white, New Haven, Conn.*

Teenage girls of every ethnic group are having sex.
— *R., black female, Greenville, S.C.*

[White girls] seem to think being sexually aggressive and outrageous will get them the most popular guys. A perfect example are Girls Gone Wild videos. It's always white girls flashing their breasts. Their parents must be so proud.
— *T.M., 36, white female, Indiana*

We found:

We assume TJ is talking about younger females, so here are some statistics:

— The Centers for Disease Control's surveys since 1991 have found that black females in grades 9-12 are more likely to report having had sexual intercourse than Hispanic and white students. In the latest findings, 61.2 percent of black girls in those grades reported ever having had sexual intercourse, compared with 44.4 percent of Hispanic girls and 43.7 percent of white girls. Meanwhile, 18.6 percent of black teen females reported having had sex with four or more persons in their life, compared with 11.1 percent for whites and 10.4 percent for Hispanics.

— However, more white female teens than girls of other races report having had more sexual experiences that fall short of intercourse. For example, among all female teens ages 15-19, whites were twice as likely to report this than African-Americans were, and 50 percent more likely than Hispanics, according to a CDC report.

Some thoughts on all this from Jennifer Manlove, senior research scientist who studies teen sexuality for the Washington, D.C.-based Child Trends, a non-profit, non-partisan research center focusing on youth issues:

White teen girls actually now report being more sexually active than their white male counterparts — but the reverse is true for other races.

"That may give the impression that white girls are more likely to have sex because they've 'caught up' with the boys in sexual experience," she said.

That, combined with the fact that white girls more often engage in sexual practices that nonetheless fall short of intercourse, such as oral sex, may create the impression in males (of any race) that white girls are more promiscuous, Manlove noted.

With respect to teen sex overall, poverty increases the chances of having sexual activity at an earlier age, and because poverty hits African Americans harder, that may partly account for higher sexual activity rates, she said.

In poverty-level households, teens' activities are, unfortunately, less likely to be as closely monitored, Manlove said.

"For teens whose parents tell them very clearly not to engage in sex, it makes it less likely they will."

'Class' warfare coming from rich white women?

They asked:

Why do a lot of upper-class suburban females have a stuck-up attitude when lower- or middle-class dudes (mostly Latinos or blacks) try to talk to them?

— Nick, Latino, Dallas

You said:

Please. You live in America, where money is king.

— E.D., 48, black female, Missouri

There's a perception that girls who get hit on by blacks and Hispanics are seen as an easy target (for sex): unattractive, overweight, poor, undereducated, etc. I guess these rich white girls are saying that being with you might make them seem not good enough to their friends.

— Corey, 35, male, Dallas

A lot of upper middle-class suburban white girls are insulated. You know how girls tend to marry someone just like Dad? Well, Daddy is a stockbroker.

— Allison, 40, Seattle

Many of today's upper-income women have educated themselves and have positions that pay good money. A woman running from meeting to meeting does not have time for idle chit-chat.

— Rhonda, 42, black, New York

These women are attracted to "success," which means that a man can carry a formidable household. It's in their nature as subconscious mothers.

— Nelson, 35, Venezuela

I grew up in a rich neighborhood and married a black man. Why? Because he treated me right. He may not have finished high school, but he is the most intelligent person I know.

— Ericka, 36, white, San Diego

We found:

Before her breakout novels "Commencement" and "Maine," best-selling author and feminist J. Courtney Sullivan interviewed more than 100 men and women on this topic for her book "Dating Up: Dump the Schlump and Find a Quality Man."

A subtle approach works best with the sophisticated lady, she found.

"Saying cheesy pick-up lines like 'I'm glad I just learned the name of the most beautiful woman in this bar' won't work," said Sullivan, whose novel "The Engagements" was purchased for a major motion picture to be produced by Reese Witherspoon. "For a certain type of woman, like me, you need to feel as if someone is just trying to have a conversation with you."

While women she interviewed were more apt to shun men perceived as financial also-rans, they usually judged income as just one part of an overall "class" package that includes chivalry, education, confidence, goals, etc.

"It seems snotty for a woman to say she doesn't want to date outside her class, but in terms of looking further down the road, if being of a different class is going to be fine when they have kids and a mortgage, that's OK, but if it's going to be an issue, they need to talk about it up front."

And while some women squirm about interracial dating, most she interviewed didn't view it as a make-or-break issue upon meeting someone.

"It's mostly the other things — approach, manners, respect — that matter."

27

You want mustard with that? Whites 'smelly' like a deli?

They asked:

Where did the statement "white people smell like bologna" originate?

— *S. May, 38, white female, Toronto*

You said:

It most likely has to do with diet. For instance, Italians (of which I'm one) have a tendency to smell like garlic because there is a lot of garlic in our food.

— *Dave L., 31, New York*

White people do have a "lunch meat" smell when they haven't bathed or are sweating heavily. When I'm in the gym with black friends, the difference in smell is noticeable.

— *Brian, 26, white, Indiana*

I never noticed whites have a smell. I do know blacks have a smell I can't seem to place. I notice it from other blacks when they sweat or don't bathe.

— *Cedric, 28, black, Jersey City, NJ.*

When backpacking, my own odor changes after a few weeks on a low-meat, high-cheese diet — to a sour smell, like old yogurt.

— *Butterfly, 30, female, Belgium*

We found:

Note to non-white people: A comparison to prosciutto drizzled with balsamic vinegar and aged olive oil would be much preferred.

The bologna thing apparently came up in the Wayans brothers' 1992 comedy-action flick "Mo' Money," and we debated renting it just to make sure. But why waste time when it's such a bland expression, anyway, and sidesteps the much spicier and well-known "white people smell like wet dogs" analogy?

Here's what people in the know about smelly things have to say:

— Pulitzer Prize-winning author David K. Shipler, who wrote "A Country of Strangers: Blacks and Whites in America": People use various ways to describe other races as unclean, etc. "It's typical in the panoply of images between racial, ethnic, national and religious groups to include lack of cleanliness and subhuman, animal analogies," he says.

— Jerome Z. Litt, dermatologist and body-odor researcher at Case Western Reserve University: People get "nose fatigue" — their nose gets used to odors of people from their own race while at the same time is sensitive to smells of people from a different cultural group. "When it comes to body odor, it's in the nose of the beholder."

— Organic chemist George Preti, body-odor expert at the Monell Chemical Senses Center in Philadelphia: While strong spices like curry and cumin might add to body odor, that hasn't been proven, and nothing points to meats adding to body odor. Also, while whites and African Americans have more bacteria-producing armpit glands than Asians, "It's been pretty well demonstrated that everybody on the planet probably produces a similar group of underarm odors."

Pimento loaf, anyone?

Does the beat go on for white people on the dance floor?

They asked:

I've noticed white people don't have rhythm when it comes to dancing. Why is this?

— Janice, 22, Atlanta

You said:

I've seen black toddlers two-stepping to hip-hop six months after learning to walk. The parents encourage it. Black people get introduced to rhythmic dancing at an early age.

— Eric, 29, white, Kansas City, Mo.

White boys tend to find interest in music that doesn't have [good] beats so it's really hard to dance to. Try doing a Kid 'N Play to Metallica. Now, if you're a white boy like me who listens to all types of music, we can bump an' grind with all the beautiful sisters.

— J.B., 23, Bridgeton, N.J.

Most white people seem to move to the 1 and 3 beats rather than the more rhythmically pleasing 2 and 4 beats.

— Heidi, 32, white, Durham, N.C.

White kids never watch BET. Where are they going to learn to dance?

— Kira, black female, Willingboro, N.J.

Eminem can dance to rap, but I bet you he couldn't line dance. It's not what a certain race can or can't do but what the individual can or can't.

— Anna, 17, white, Memphis, Tenn.

It's more acceptable in the African-American community for people to take risks in making themselves look stupid. So dancing is more easily passed from one generation to the next.

— Jessica, 18, white, Chicago

Maybe white people are less self-conscious or get drunker quicker, so they dance even if they know they're no good.

— *Milly, white, London*

We found:

We put this one to exceedingly white dancing phenom Wade Robson, a "So You Think You Can Dance?" judge; creative director for Demi Lovato; and choreographer for Britney Spears, 'N Sync, Usher and others. (Side note: Robson's abuse allegations against Michael Jackson when Robson was a child are the subject of the documentary "Leaving Neverland.")

"I guess like other traits, race has nothing to do with it at the core," he said, missing nary a beat. "It depends on what you grow up listening to and watching."

But this guy has taught thousands to shake it and kick it, so allow him his generalizations:

"I find black people have more of a natural funk and feeling and vibe, but that they have more trouble picking up the steps, and vice versa [for white people]. ... Culturally speaking, black people tend more to grow up watching movies, videos, going to clubs with friends, and it's more about improvisation. White people tend to put their kids in classes early on — ballet, jazz, etc. — so they tend to be more technically driven."

And what exactly makes a good dancer, anyway?

"It's not about cockiness, it's about a carefree feeling," Robson said. "I've seen dorky white dudes get up and don't care and have a blast. Maybe they're not the funkiest on the block, but they let their passion come through. You can be technically great, but if you're inhibited, you'll look dorkier than someone who doesn't have talent but doesn't care."

Nosing around about those picky people

They asked:

I notice sometimes when I'm driving or going for a walk that white people dig in their noses. Why do they do this?
> — *Simone, 20, black female, White Plains, N.Y.*

You said:

What do you do with your boogers? Put them in a crystal case and mail them to the Queen of England?
> — *Justin, white, Chicago*

My grown sister does this all the time. It's just a bad habit. I did have a white junior high teacher who was known for picking her nose; pretty nasty. I've also seen people dig up their ears and other things, but you and I both know it's not a cultural thing.
> — *Lisa, black, Gaithersburg, Md.*

I think it's just lax standards in the workplace. My very Caucasian boss not only picks his nose, he scratches his crotch and butt, and generally behaves in a manner I would normally associate with a high school dropout or truck driver.
> — *Ann, 38, white, Kansas City, Mo.*

Maybe [Asian picking is] just something there's less taboo about. On the other hand, eating with your fingers revolts many Chinese.
> — *Adrian, 36, white, Hong Kong*

We found:

Our research turned up experts on white culture and Asian culture. We found experts on nose-picking. But we couldn't find any on white or Asian nose-picking.

Garden variety nose-picking hasn't been studied much. In an article for Psychology Today, Dr. Mark Griffiths, a psychologist at

Nottingham Trent University (UK), wrote: "Nose-picking on the face of it (no pun intended) is probably one of the most under-researched activities given the fact that it is an every-day activity for many people and appears to be a universal activity across cultures. It is believed that across many cultures, nose-picking belongs to a set of behaviors considered a private act (such as burping, farting, urinating and defecating)."

However, in terms of research, rhinotillexomania, or compulsive nose-picking, is another story. It's been studied much more often. (We won't get into mucophagy. Thank us.)

James Jefferson and Trent Thompson of the University of Wisconsin Medical School surveyed people about their nose-picking and published their seminal results in The Journal of Clinical Psychiatry.

Let's drill down into the numbers, shall we?

Of 254 respondents, 91 percent were classified (using technical jargon) as "current nose-pickers." Thus apparently all races and ethnicities are welcome to the club.

8.7 percent said they never picked their nose. That is, they were "Big Liars."

About one in four pick daily. Half spend one to five minutes per day doing it; 83 percent go mining to "unclog the nasal passages." And 2 percent do it just for fun.

The researchers' conclusion? "This first population survey of nose-picking suggests it is an almost universal practice in adults, but one that should not be considered pathologic for most."

Meanwhile, Dr. Chittaranjan Andrade and Dr. B.S. Srihari of the National Institute of Mental Health and Neurosciences in Bangalore, India, studied 200 adolescents and reported in the Journal of Clinical Psychiatry that they picked their noses about four times a day.

Put that in your proboscis and smoke it.

The O.U.T.L.O.U.D. Method to Dialogue

OPEN UP: This is mostly about opening up to yourself. Why do you want to engage someone? Is it for the right reasons? The answers might help you figure out how to approach another person. A friend once told me the real reason I started Y? wasn't for me to learn more about "Buddhists in Asia or lesbians in San Francisco," but because I wanted to learn something more about myself. He was right. Acknowledging that has helped give me perspective when considering others' answers.

USE YOUR HEAD: Plan for the right question. Not all questions need to be the "wet dogs" variety. Stereotypes and clichés don't work as well as sincere attempts to talk.

TIME IT RIGHT: Create the "O.U.T.L.O.U.D. Moment". Pick your spots for provocative dialogue. Find a genuine opening rather than create a false one. It's often during those down times between all the "vital" discourse that we can most easily find a direct path to someone's point of view. If you spend enough time sitting in the cubicle next to someone of a different culture, chances are there'll come a time — over food, perhaps, or during a power outage — when the topic you've been dying to broach will wend its way naturally into the discussion.

LOCK IN ON THE TARGET: Keeping things simple can give the best chance for getting another's trust and a meaningful reply. Some of the best questions at Y?, those that prompt the most telling answers, are also often the easiest to digest. Remember, it's not about winning your point. It's what comes from the heart that counts most — and captures people's interest. Talking from the heart also means easing into things by letting someone know *why* it would help you to learn the answer to your question before you ask it.

OWN UP TO ASSUMPTIONS: One of the most refreshing and repetitive surprises of the Y? project is the difficulty in predicting how a person will respond to a question. Blacks do not think in lockstep. Nor do whites. Nor Christians or Muslims. Nor gays or straights. Be receptive to another's ideas. Wipe the slate clean and listen to the content of the message, not the color or culture of the messenger.

UNLOAD YOUR EXPECTATIONS: Many of us are thinner-skinned than we'll admit. When we get hit with an answer or comment we hadn't anticipated, our emotions can often get caught off-balance, and our egos get bruised. The solution: Expect the unexpected. You'll never be blindsided or taken aback by information that doesn't gibe with your worldview.

DIGEST THE DIALOGUE: Learning about others doesn't stop when the talking's over. Assess what you're told and how it fits with or departs from your perspectives. Recap your discussion with a third party to distill the most relevant information into its most meaningful points.

ABOUT THE AUTHOR

Phillip J. Milano is the founder of Y? The National Forum on People's Differences, the acclaimed cross-cultural dialogue project that encourages people to ask unflinching, politically incorrect questions about our differences.

Since its creation in 1998, Phillip's web site, YForum.com, has attracted millions of visitors and thousands of questions and answers. He has been featured on CBS, CNN, BET and the BBC, and in numerous newspapers, including The Washington Post, New York Times and USA Today.

He is the author of the Perigee book "I Can't Believe You Asked That!" as well as writer of the pioneering newspaper column/blog "Dare to Ask."

Mr. Milano is a 25-year newspaper veteran. He received his Master of Business Administration from Northern Illinois University and his Bachelor of Science in Journalism from Southern Illinois University.

SPEECHES AND APPEARANCES

Mr. Milano is an in-demand speaker. For bookings, contact

Contemporary Issues Agency
809 Turnberry Drive, Waunakee, WI 53597-2256
Phone: 800-843-2179
Fax: 608-849-6311
www.CIAspeakers.com
Info@CIAspeakers.com